HOPE

A Story from the Farm

By
Storey Grace

Illustrated by
Corrie Lee

To my wonderful family and friends.
Thank ya'll!

And to Hope...
for being the best calf that a girl could
ever ask for.

Chapter One

Every girl has something from childhood that makes an unforgettable impact on her life.
What was it for you?

For me, it was a baby cow.
It may sound silly, but it's true and, yes, I am a country girl.

I was thirteen years old when my dad told me to get my boots on and go to the truck.
I immediately knew what was happening. My heart was racing as I ran to my room, put on my boots and climbed into the truck.

The ride to the farm was about an hour long and as soon as my dad stopped, I jumped out. I was so excited.

The farmer greeted us by riding over a hill on a four-wheeler with a cigarette hanging out of the side of his mouth.

"You must be here for a calf," he said as he got off of the four-wheeler and took the cigarette out of his mouth.

"Yes sir, we are," my dad said as they shook hands.

"Follow me then," said the farmer as he led us to a barn. Before opening the door, he grabbed a crate of bottles and as soon as he opened the door, the calves started making all kinds of noise. They were bawling. A wave of happiness came over me.
The barn was one big room separated into three parts by little wooden fences.

"The closer you get to the wall, the older the calves get," said the farmer as he started to feed the calves milk from the bottles.

"Here, you can feed one if ya like," he said as he handed me a bottle. I looked around the room, found a little one in the corner and began feeding her.

"Dad, I think I want this one," I said.

"Are you sure? How about you keep looking. You may change your mind," replied my dad.

I looked around and caught a glimpse of one calf sneaking out of the barn. I followed and found her jumping and running around. I smiled and said, "Dad you were right. I would like this one!"

My dad walked out of the barn and smiled, "That one is perfect."

My dad paid the farmer. Then he tried to put the calf in the truck. First of all, she didn't want to be shoved into a truck, and secondly, she wasn't the lightest calf. After a few tries, my dad finally got her into the truck. I crawled onto the seat next to her, my dad got into the driver's seat and we were off.

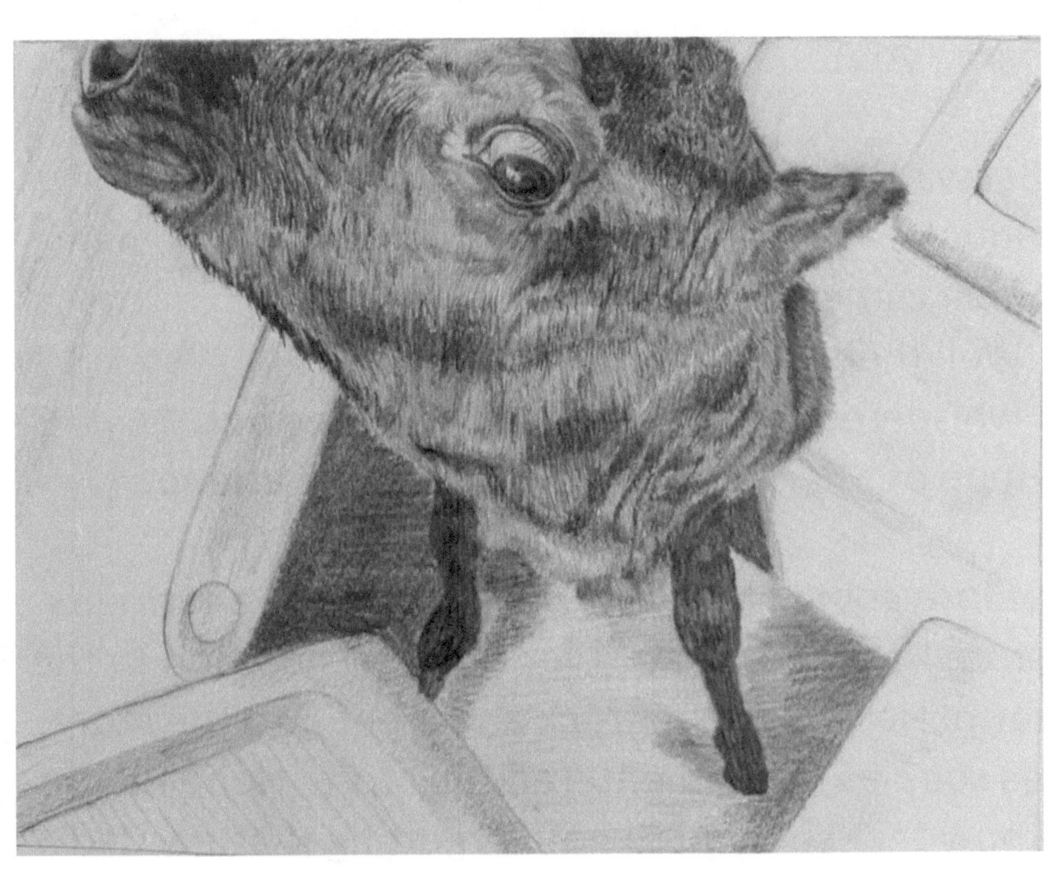

I studied my calf and saw that she had a white spot on her leg that looked like a heart. Her belly was white and she had a white spot on her head. She had big brown eyes and a little cute nose. As I looked her over I thought, "What am I going to name you?"

Bessy? Hope? River? Rose? Faith? Lily? Kate? Hmmm. I looked into her eyes and again the name Hope came to me.
"Well then, your name is Hope."
I whispered into her ear, "Hope, I love you."
Hope put her head on my lap and fell asleep.

Before going home, my dad stopped at a farmer's store to get some stuff for our new addition to the farm. He locked the truck and went into the store. As soon as my dad entered the store, Hope let me know that she had to go! Forgetting that my dad had locked the door from the outside, I quickly opened the door. Big mistake. The alarm went off which scared Hope and made her go crazy. My dad ran out of the store, turned off the alarm and then he went back inside.

I pulled Hope out of the truck and she pooped right in the middle of the parking lot! We went around to the back of the truck and I let down the tail gate. Lifting her up was not easy! I realized how heavy she was but finally got her up there. There was a cage in the back of the truck and I pushed her inside.
My dad finally came out of the store.
I thought he had bought the whole store.

"Do we really need all this stuff?" I asked.
"You can never be too prepared," he said.

I shut the door to the cage, jumped down from the tailgate, got into the truck and off we drove. We didn't get too far, though. Hope was slipping and sliding in her cage. That was not going to work! My dad stopped in a turning lane, got out, took Hope out of the cage and put her back into the tuck. As we pulled into the driveway to our house, everyone came out to see what we were bringing home. After everyone had seen her, dad and I took her to the barn and put her into a stall that was prepared for her. My dad left me with Hope.

I watched Hope nuzzle down in a pile of hay and something happened to me. A warm feeling came over me. I was happy. I finally had my calf.

Again, I whispered "I love you, Hope."

Then I left the barn.

Chapter Two

The next day I thought Hope was going to die. She was laying down and not moving so I got my mom up to the barn and we brought her to the house. I got a tarp out and put it in our den. We found out she was sick because we had fed her too much. Hope and I spent the day outside walking around and inside watching cheesy romance movies. The only thing I didn't like about the day was when I had to clean up her messes (she had a lot of those). Later that day I took her back up to the barn. As she nestled down into a warm spot, a smile broke across my face.

I whispered, "I love you, Hope," and with that, I left the barn.

The days flew by and I got into a rhythm of doing things. I would walk up to the barn, feed the goats, water the cows and then I would go back to the barn and feed Hope. She would be bawling her head off until the bottle was in her mouth. When she finished the bottle, she would suck on my fingers. It was heartwarming to see her ready for her bottle every day. I told her all my life problems and she would just suck my finger or follow me if I was walking around her stall. I would whisper "I love you, Hope," before I left the barn.

By the time I would get home I would be covered in milk and slobber. In the evenings, I would walk up to the barn and just feed Hope but before I left, I always whispered, "I love you, Hope".

One day my dad came up to me and told me that there was a baby bull calf whose mother had stopped feeding because she had gotten stuck in the mud and then got really sick. He asked me if I could take care of him so we could grow him up to breed with our other cows and if I took good care of him he could breed with Hope, too. I told him he had a deal and about an hour later Buddy the bull calf was in the stall with Hope.

It took about a week for him to warm up to his new home. Buddy wasn't like Hope. He was bigger and acted tougher. But when I pulled out his bottle he would do anything for it. Hope was smaller, sweeter and she made friends with anyone. Hope would always hold a special spot in my heart that Buddy never could. Yes, I loved Buddy but he wasn't like Hope.

Buddy and Hope became best of friends. They would play with each other and they ate with each other. They even slept together which was cute because Buddy would totally cover up Hope because he was so much bigger than her.

Hope did only one thing that Buddy didn't like. After they drank their bottles, Hope would suck on Buddy's ears. It was funny to watch. He would try to get away but she would follow him. Slowly but surely, they got too big for their stall. So, one day, I opened up their stall door and led them out into a goat pen. The goats where very surprised to see two cows walk out of a stall. But they didn't make a big fuss about it so everything went fine.

Chapter Three

Have you ever had someone that really bugged you?

For Hope and Buddy, it was our mini-donkey. I was eating lunch outside one time when I looked up at the goat pen to see our donkey chasing Buddy. Boy, did I get mad! I was so mad I hadn't realized that I had broken my toe nail. Before entering the goat pen I grabbed me a good-sized stick, walked up to that donkey and walloped him a good one. So good that he ran to the other side of the pen.

That day I decided to let Buddy out of the pen and let him be with the bigger cows. We had moved the big cows and buddy to a field across the lake.

The day came when I thought it was time for Hope to leave the pen too, so I got her to follow me across the lake. As soon as Buddy realized that Hope was coming to him he started to bawl. Every once in while Hope would bawl back. When I finally got Hope to Buddy he ran up to her and put his head around her neck.

One morning I noticed that Hope was coughing a lot and that she was weak. I got my dad to look at her and he said if she got worse he would call the veterinarian. The next day she could hardly stand. I sat with her for hours on end. I sang her songs. I patted her down with a wet rag. Every once in a while, I would lean close to her ear and whisper, "I love you, Hope. Everything is going to be fine".

When my dad got home from work he called the vet. The vet said she had pneumonia and that he would have shots for her tomorrow. We could pick them up, give them to her and she should get better.

The next morning it was pouring rain and I had to go find Hope to put her in a stall. I looked for about an hour and could not find her. But finally, I did! I brought her to the barn, plugged in a heating lamp and then went to get her shots. My mom helped me give her the shots. The next day my family and I

left for vacation and left my grandfather in charge
of the farm.

One day on vacation my dad walked up to me and I
knew something was wrong but I didn't say. I was
tanning on the beach with my sister when he and
my mom walked up to me.

"Dear, I am sorry but we have some bad news," said
my dad.

I immediately knew my calf was gone.
"Oh no!" I said and turned away from him.

"Your grandfather found her this morning."

I was mad. Then I was sad. Then it was a mix. I sat
down frustrated.

"You were a good mama," my mom said. I mumbled
under my breath so no one could hear, "apparently
not good enough".

My mom and dad left and I just sat there in total shock. She was gone. She was truly gone. I wanted to yell or scream. I wanted to let people know I was hurt really bad. Tears came down my face and all I wanted to do was go home.

The next morning, I woke up and walked out onto the balcony. I looked out over the ocean, sighed and imagined Hope in a field with a flower necklace that I loved to make her.

A tear rolled down my face as I remembered the news my parents had told me the day before. As a soft breeze touched my cheeks, I could feel my hands shake.

I closed my eyes and held on to the railing in front of me and heard a soft opening and shutting of the door behind me. Then I felt a soft warm hand take mine.

"Are you okay?" my sister asked.

I opened my eyes, smiled and replied, "I will be fine."

I could see the concern in her eyes as she pulled me into a hug.

Chapter Four

When we got home, I took my time unloading the car, ate something and then realized it was time to go see her. I promised myself I wouldn't cry until I got to the grave. As the grave came in sight, a lump grew in my throat. My eyes had tears in them but none fell out until I got to the grave. Standing where she was buried all of my tears fell out. I knelt down to the ground and through my tears I saw that my grandfather had planted some flowers and put a solar powered lamp by her grave.

With a weak voice, I said, "I am so sorry. I know I could have done more".

I put my hands on the grave hoping to feel something... anything... but nothing came except a wave of coldness.

As I stood up, memories came to my head. Memories like when I first saw Hope and when I last saw Hope. When I first fed her and how she sucked on my fingers. How Hope and Buddy loved each other. I was heartbroken. Tears kept rolling down my face and my hands were shaking. I couldn't believe she was gone... truly gone.

I raised her.

I loved her.

I played with her.

I fed her.

I know she will always have a special place in my heart.

I walked away from the grave, stopped, looked back and whispered, "I love you, Hope."

One more tear rolled down my face and I walked away. This time I didn't look back because hope was with me.

The End